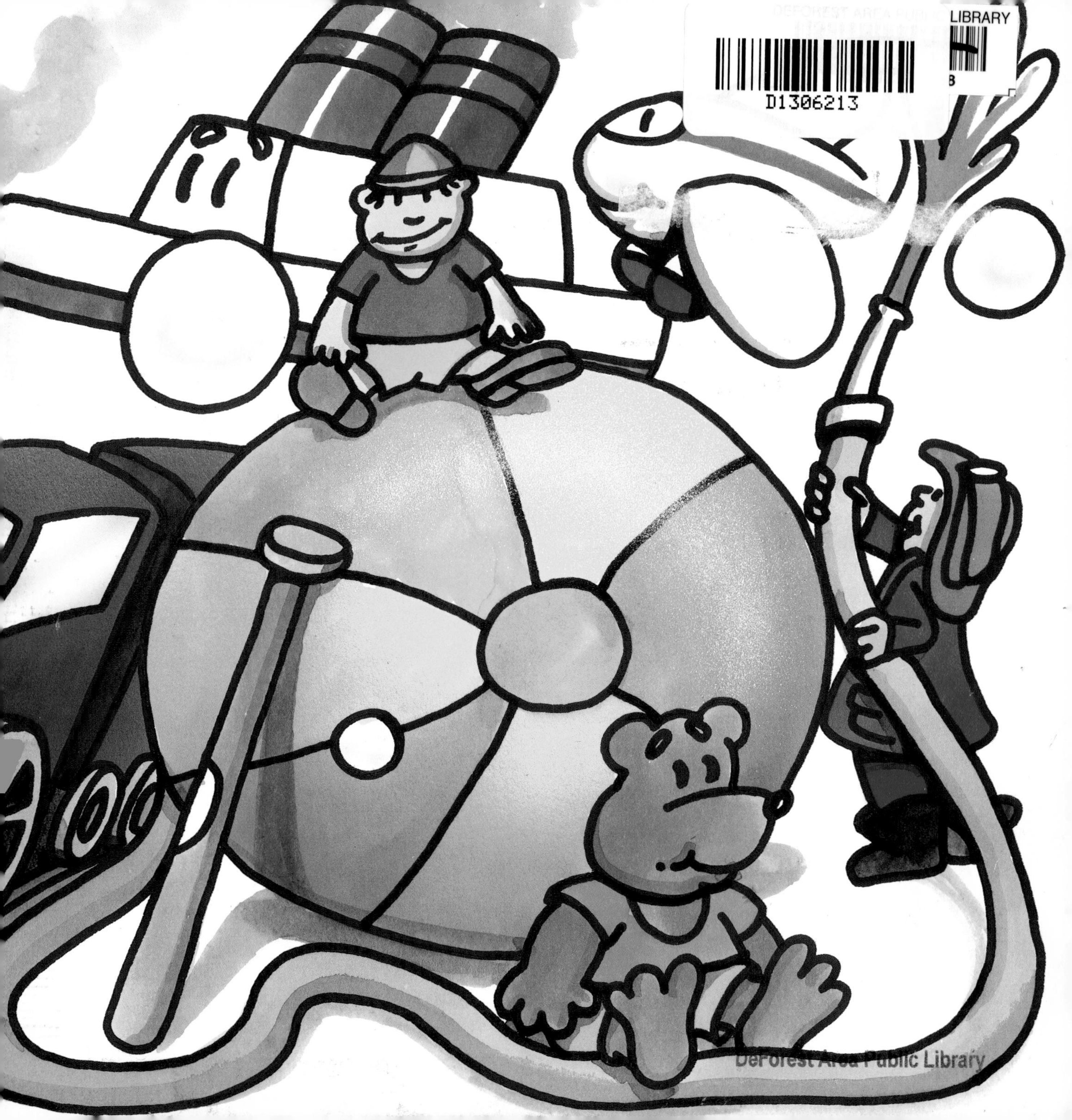

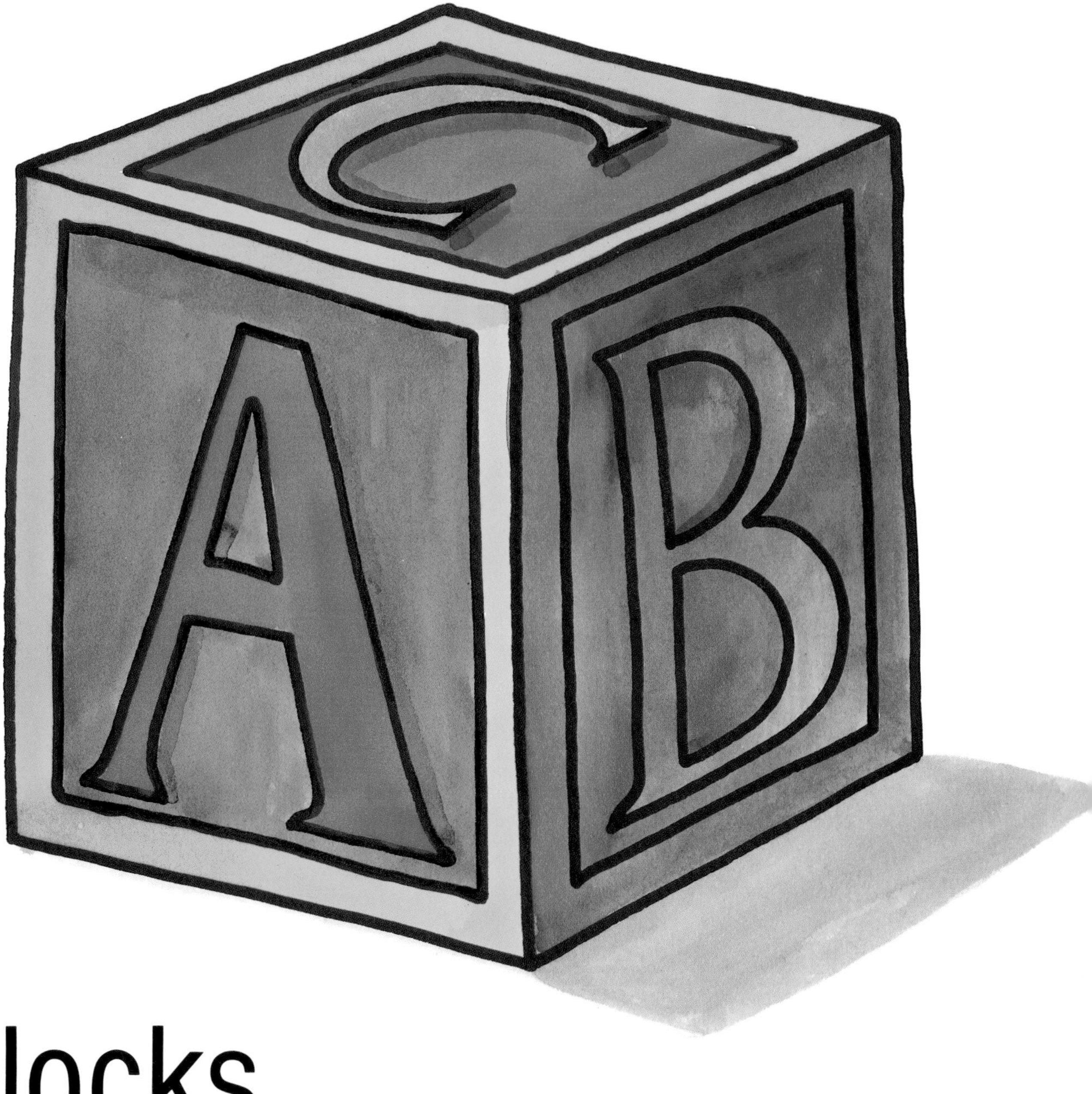

Blocks

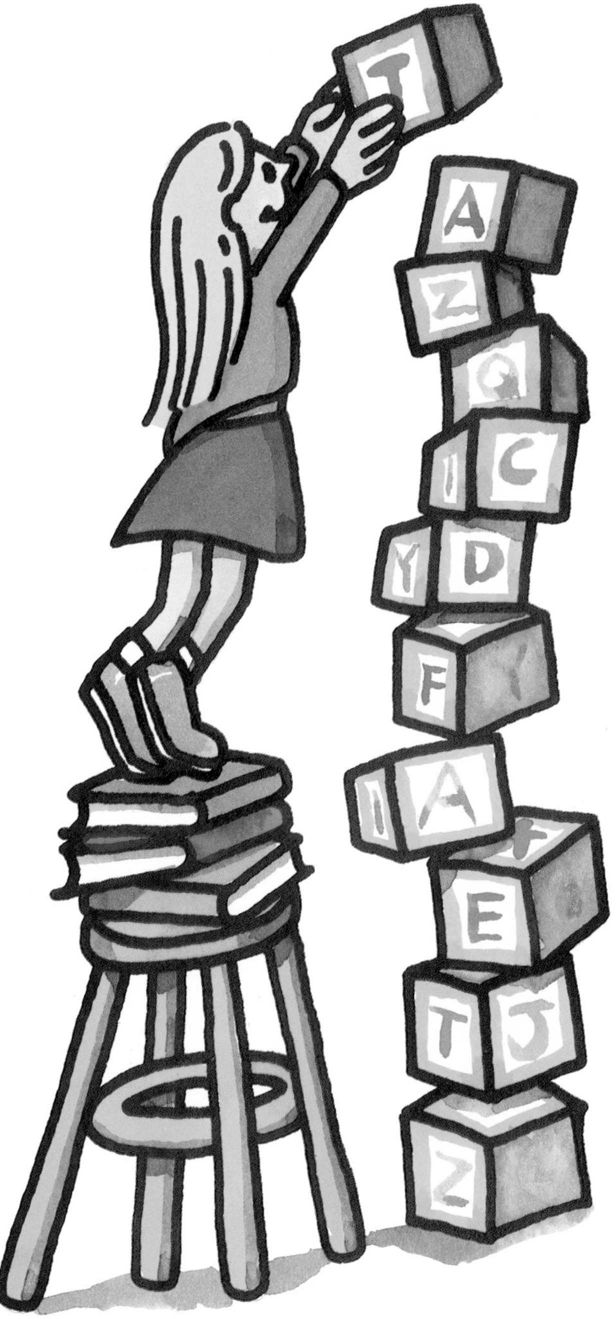

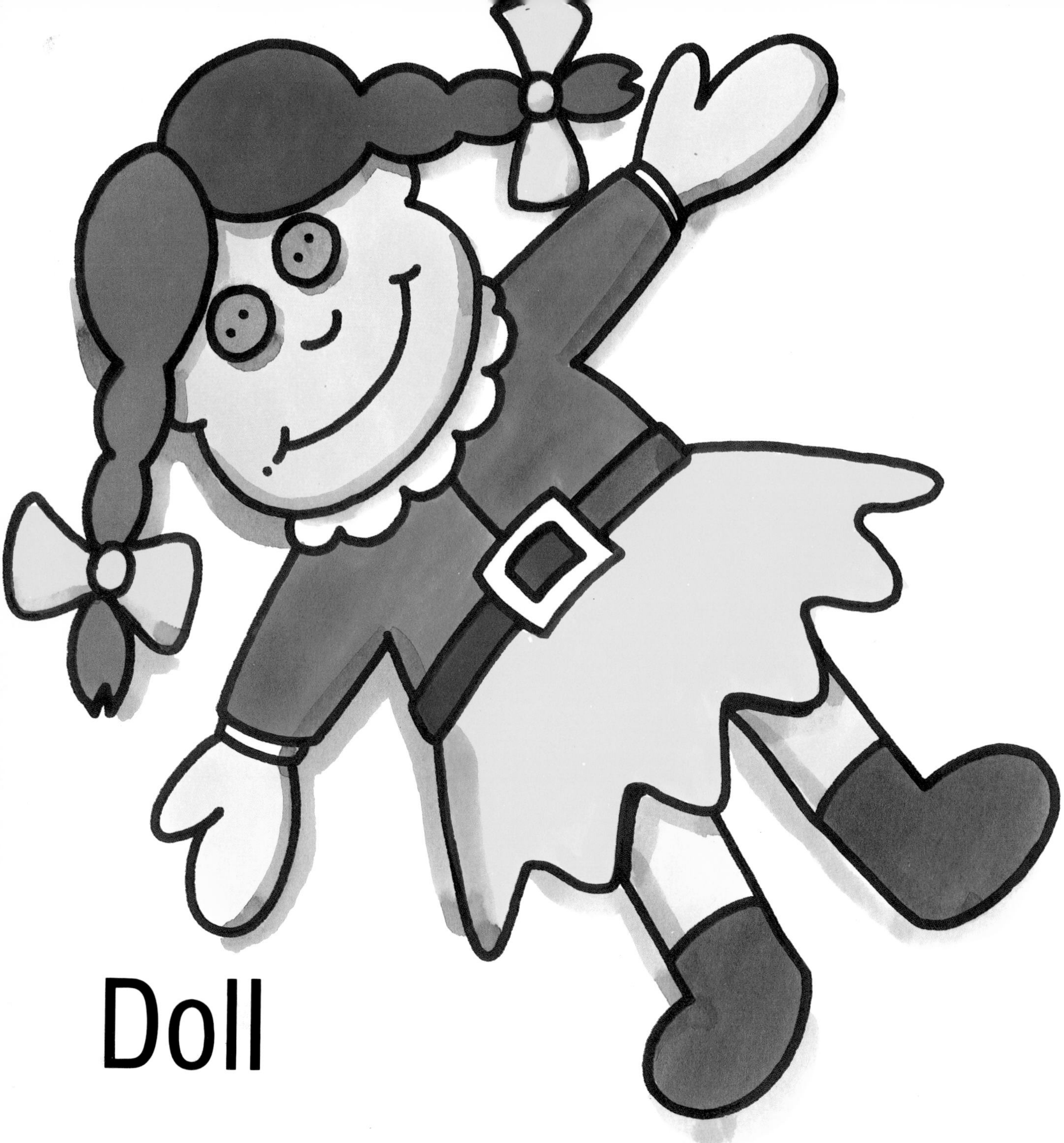

Doll

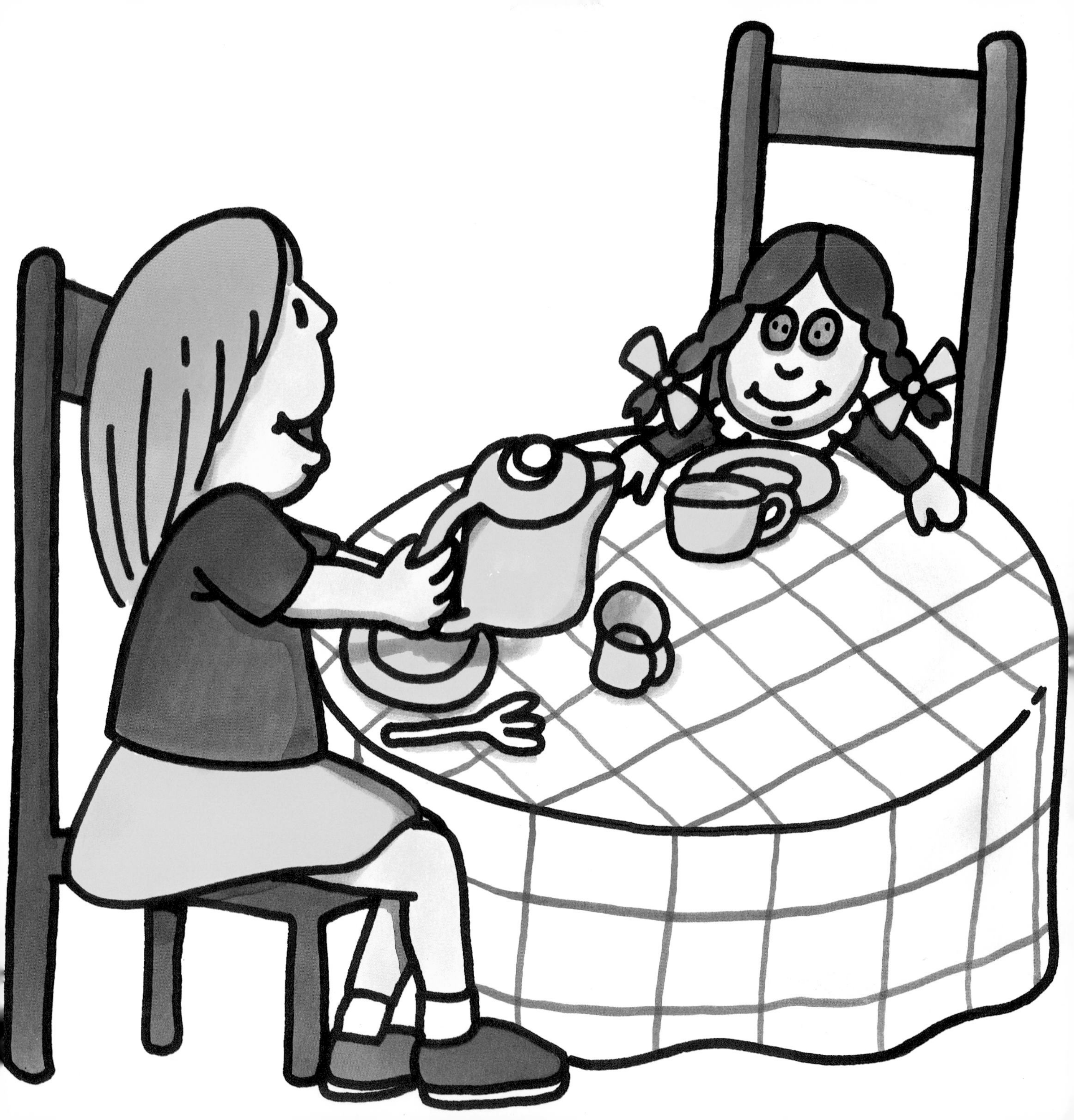

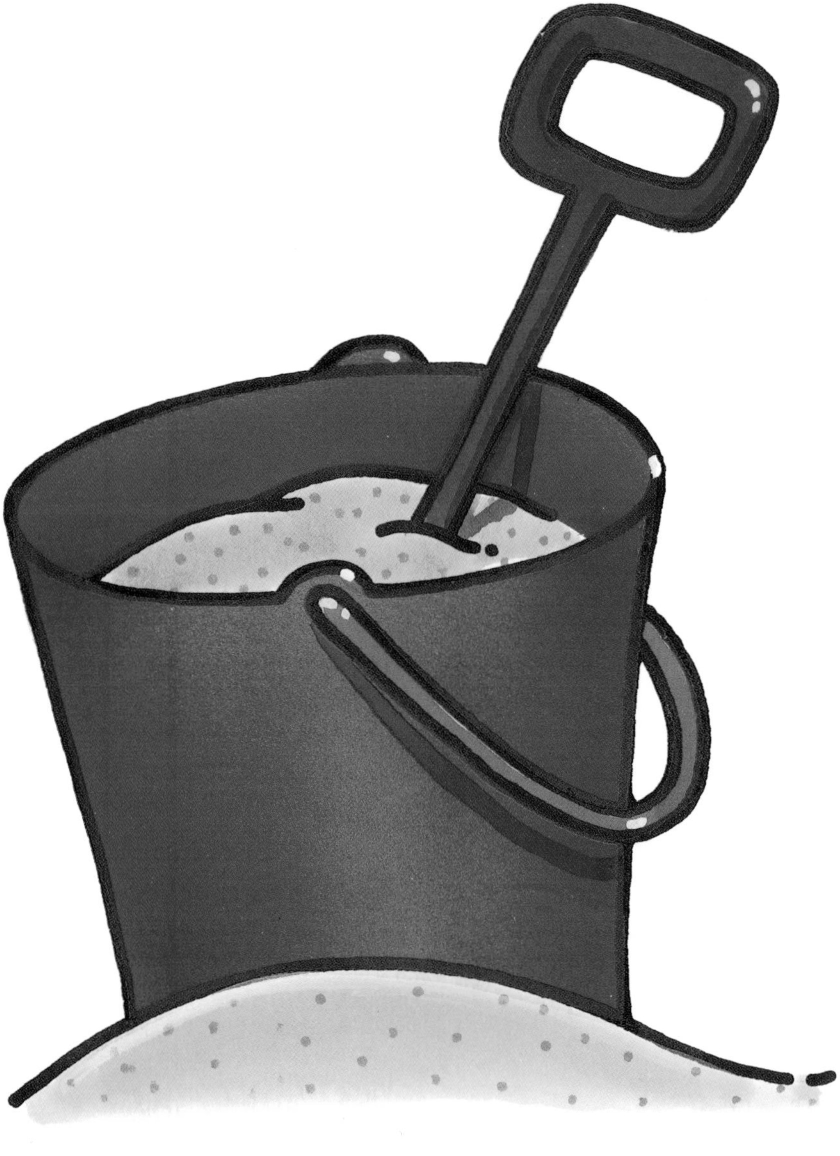

Bucket+Shovel

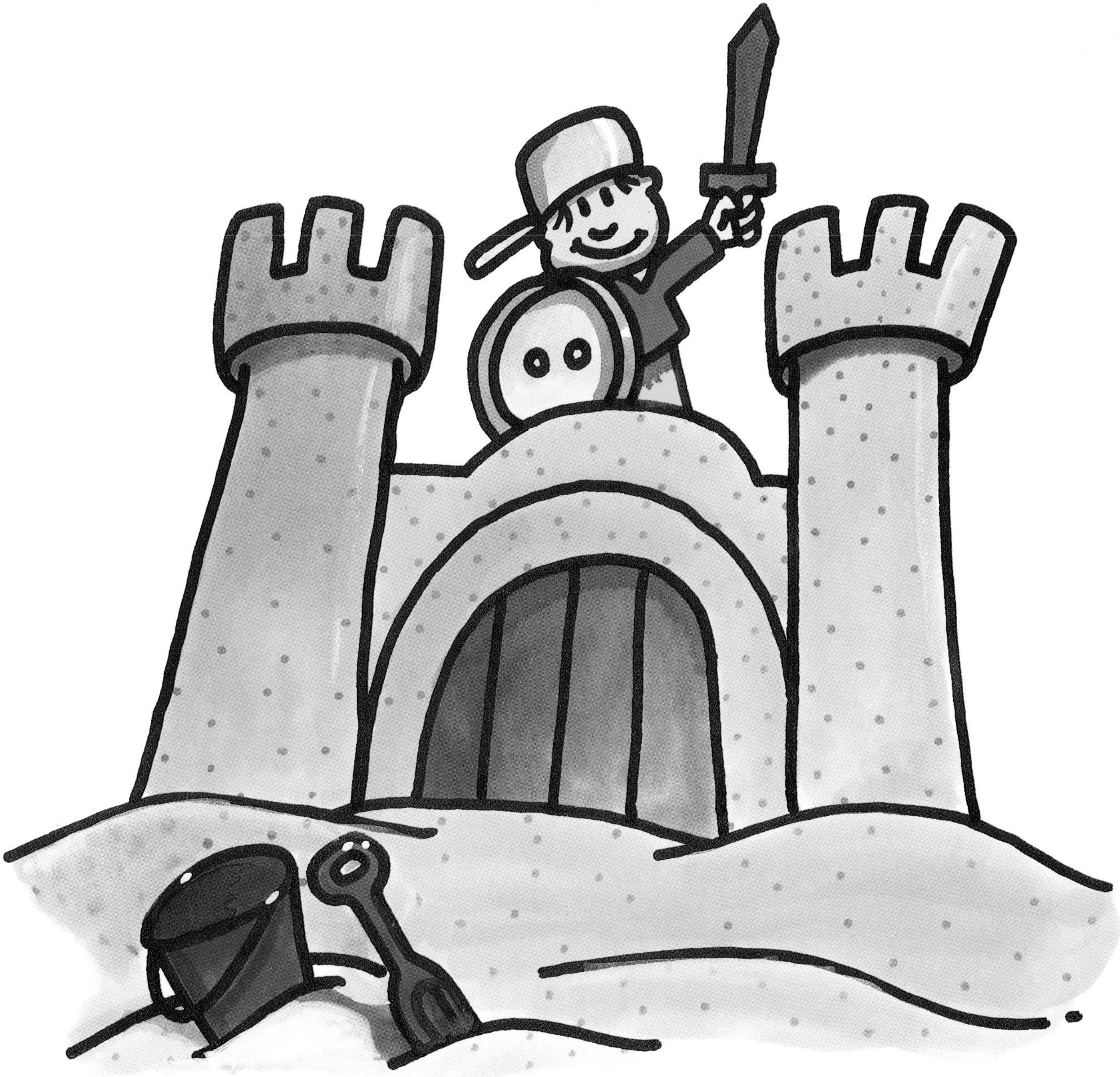

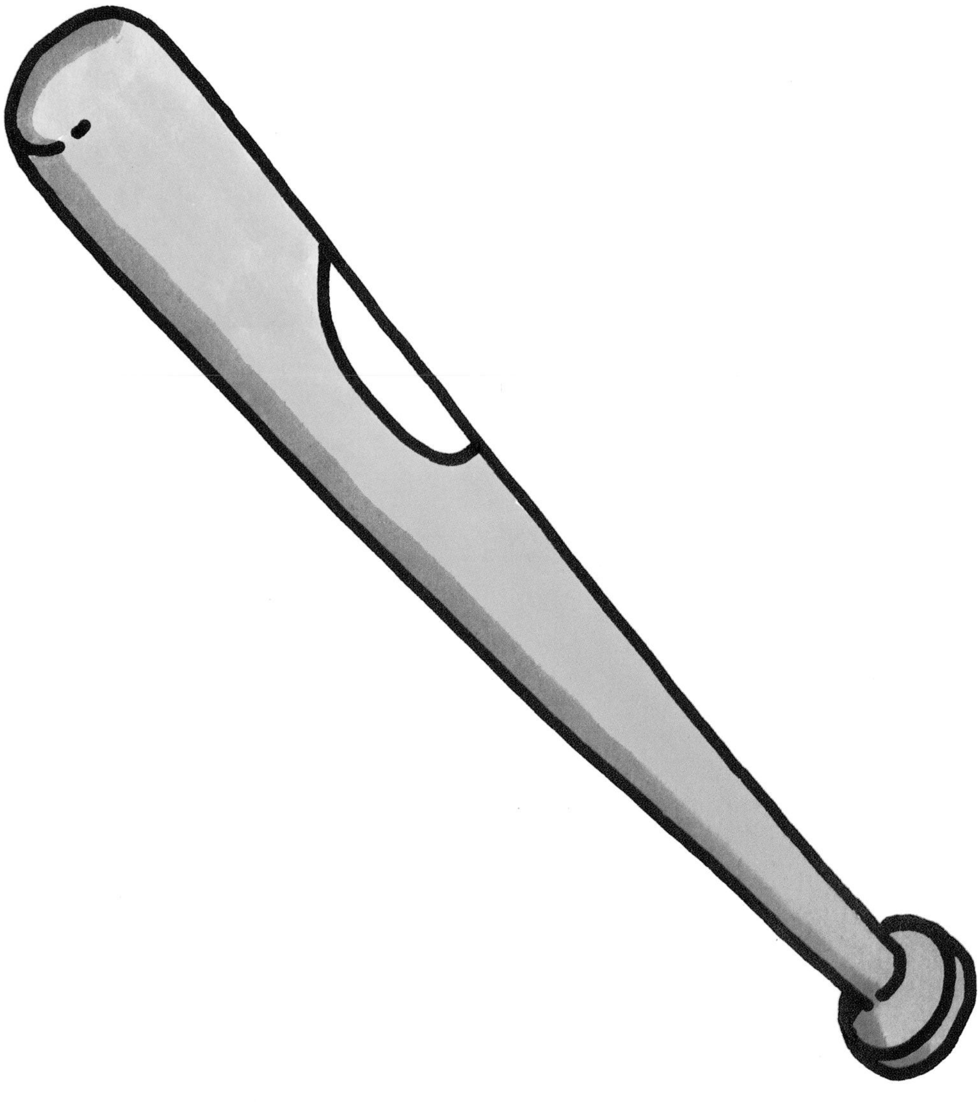

Bat

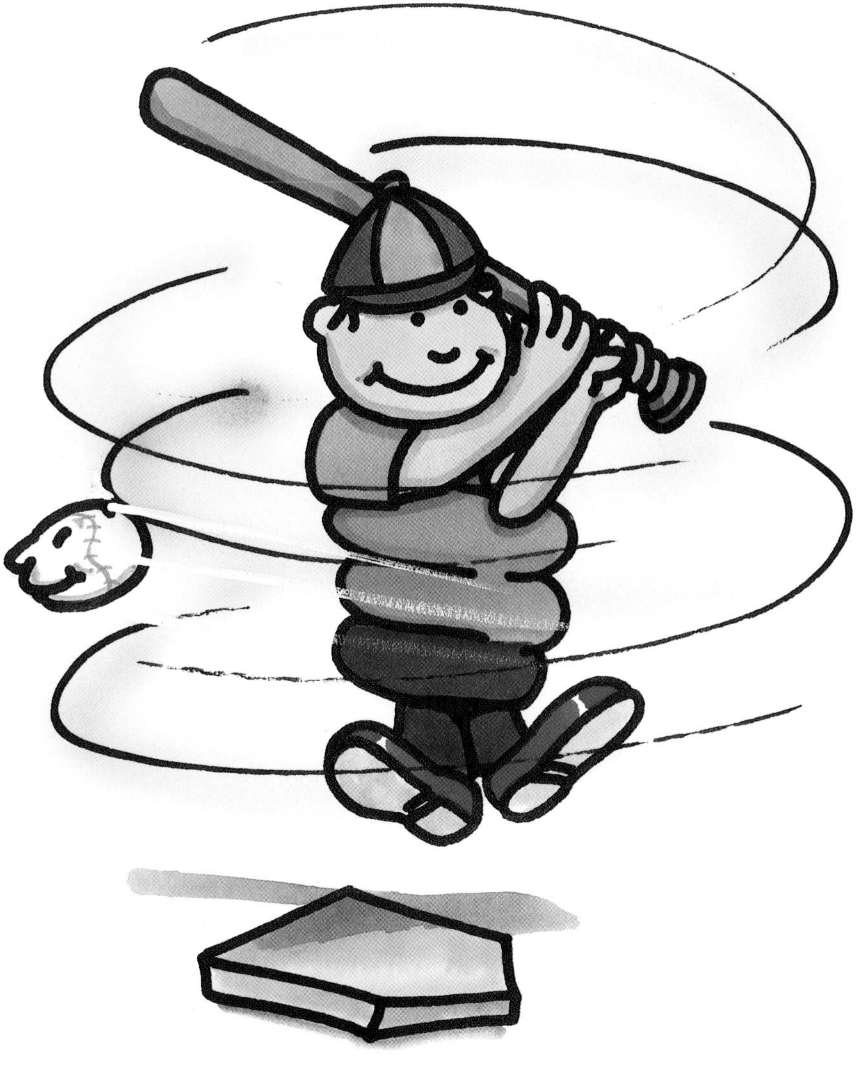

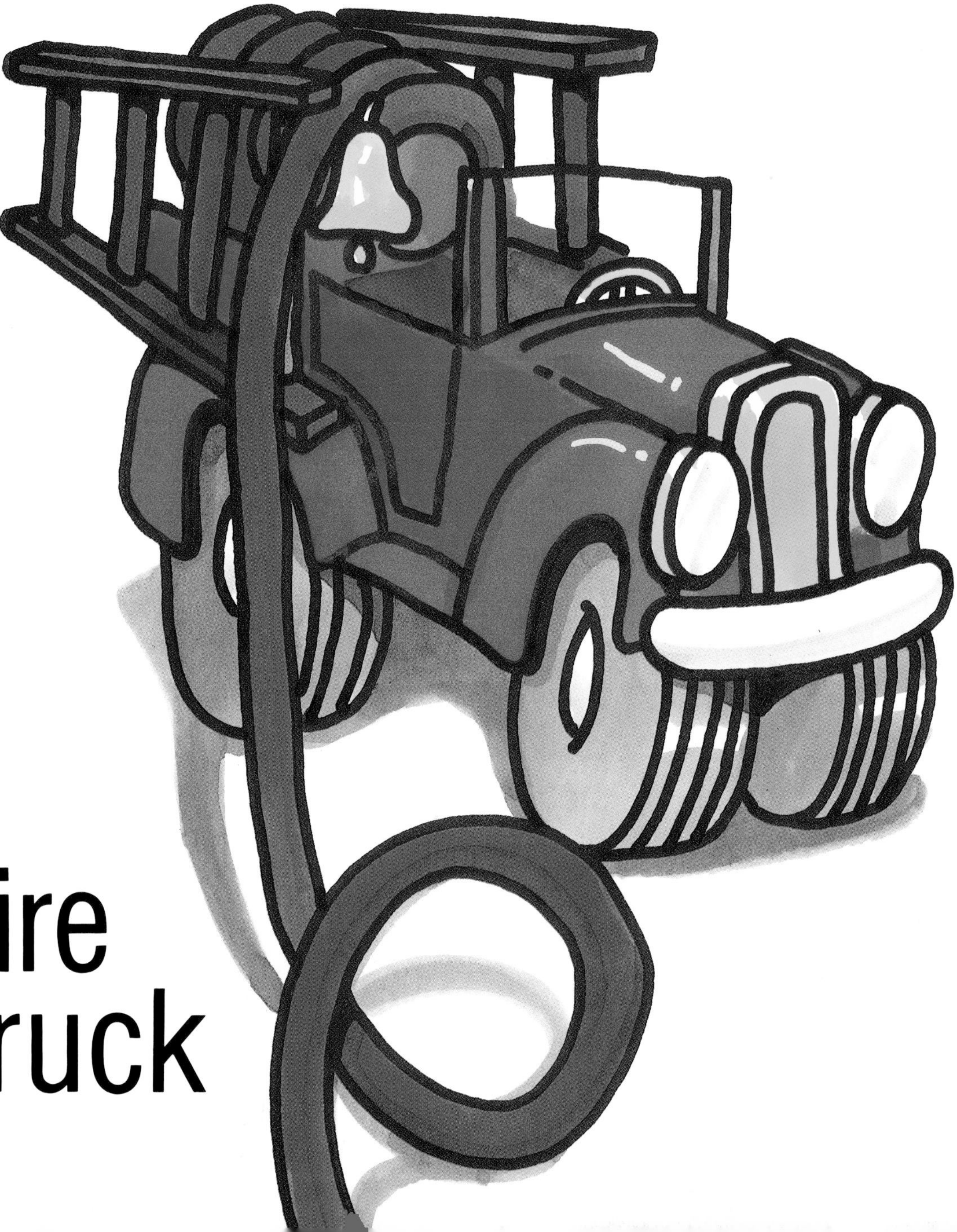

Fire Truck

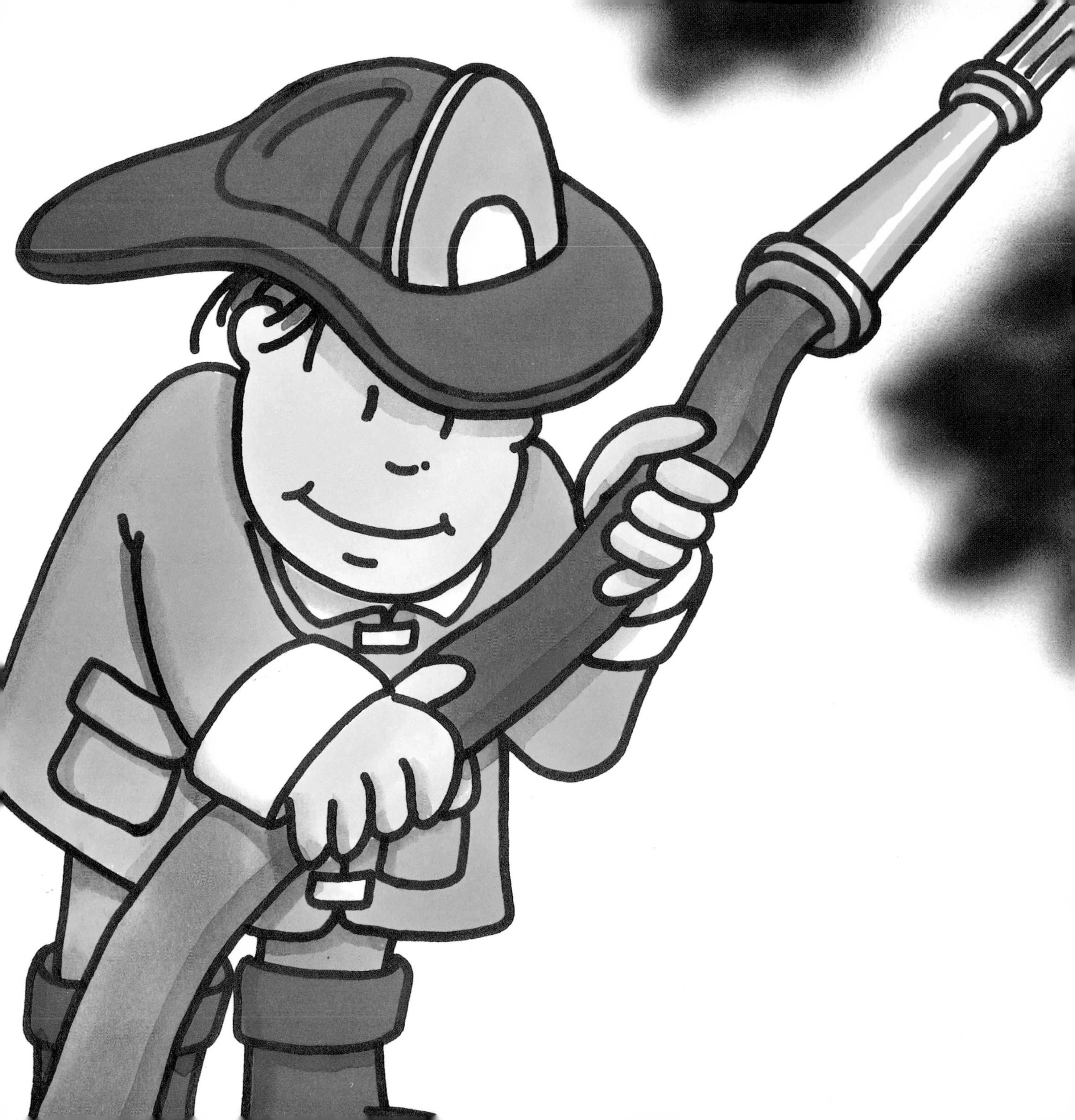

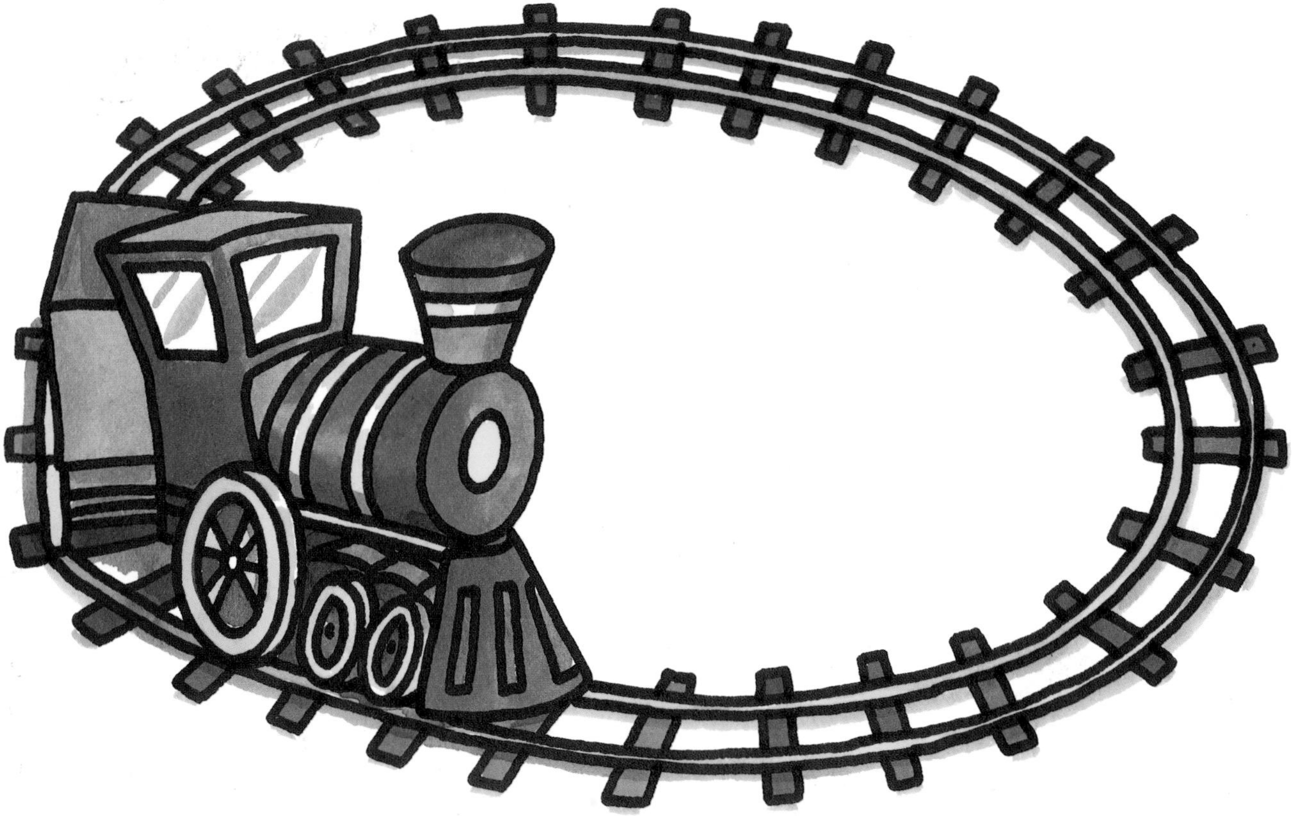

Train

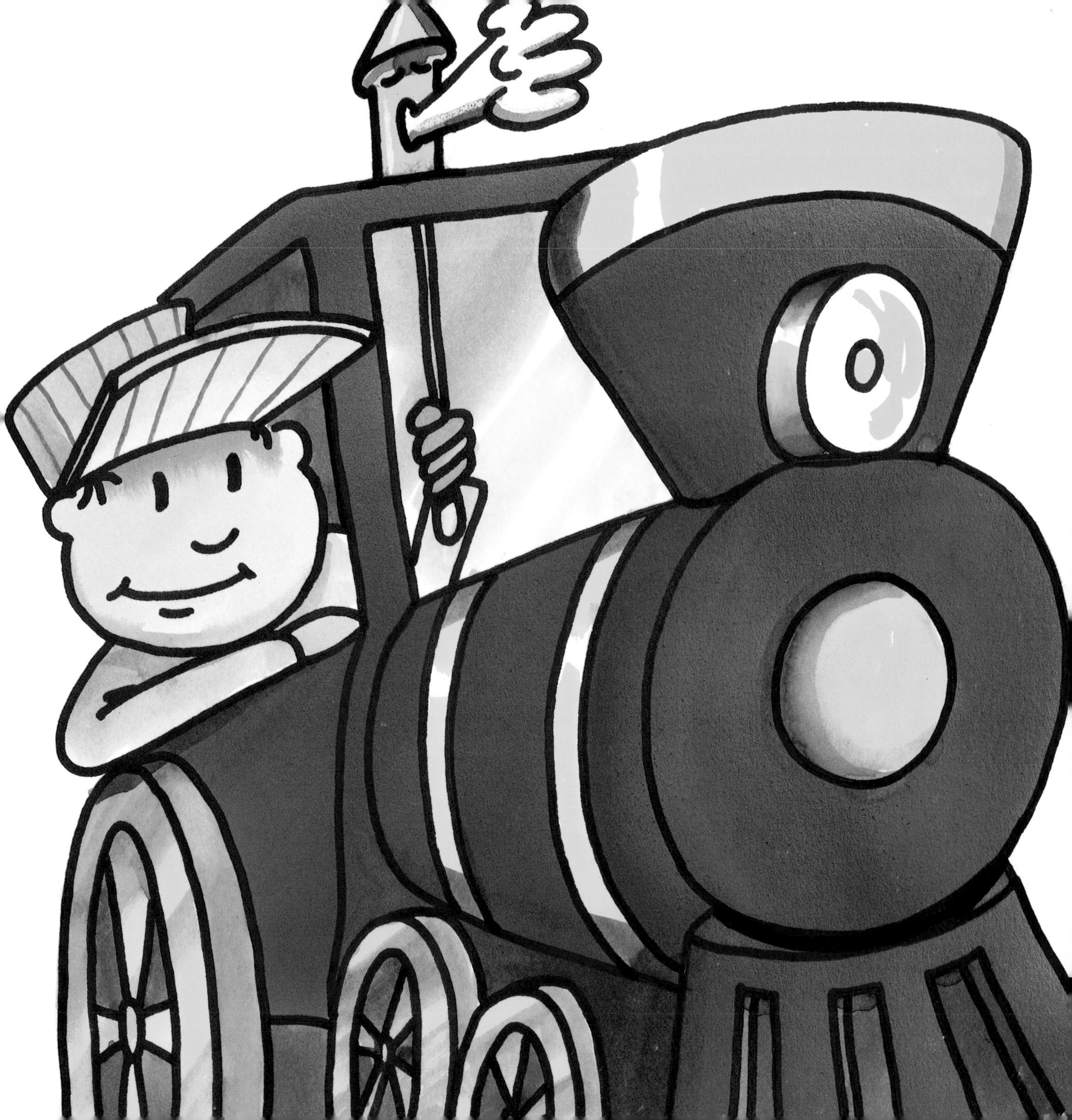

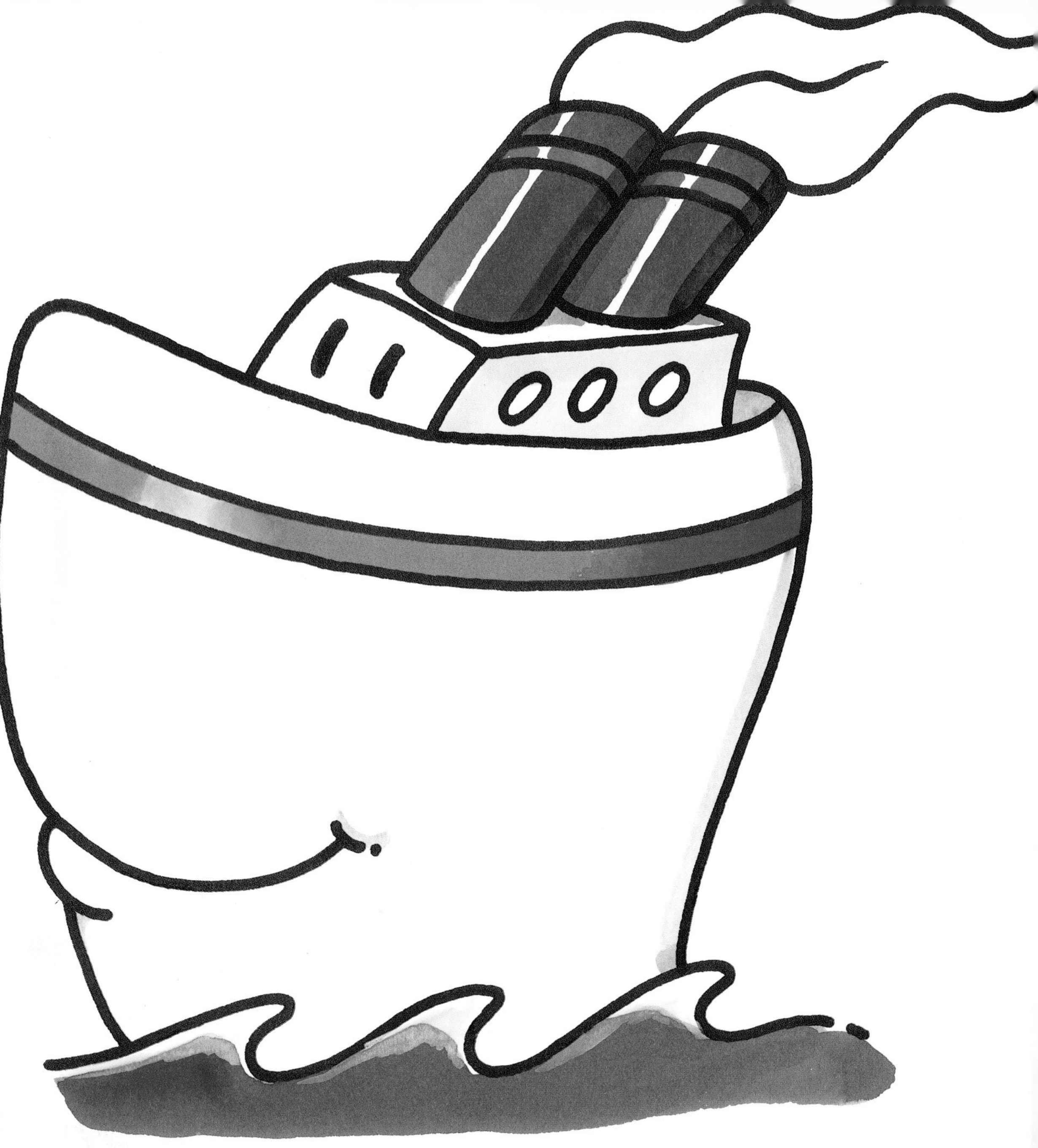

Boat

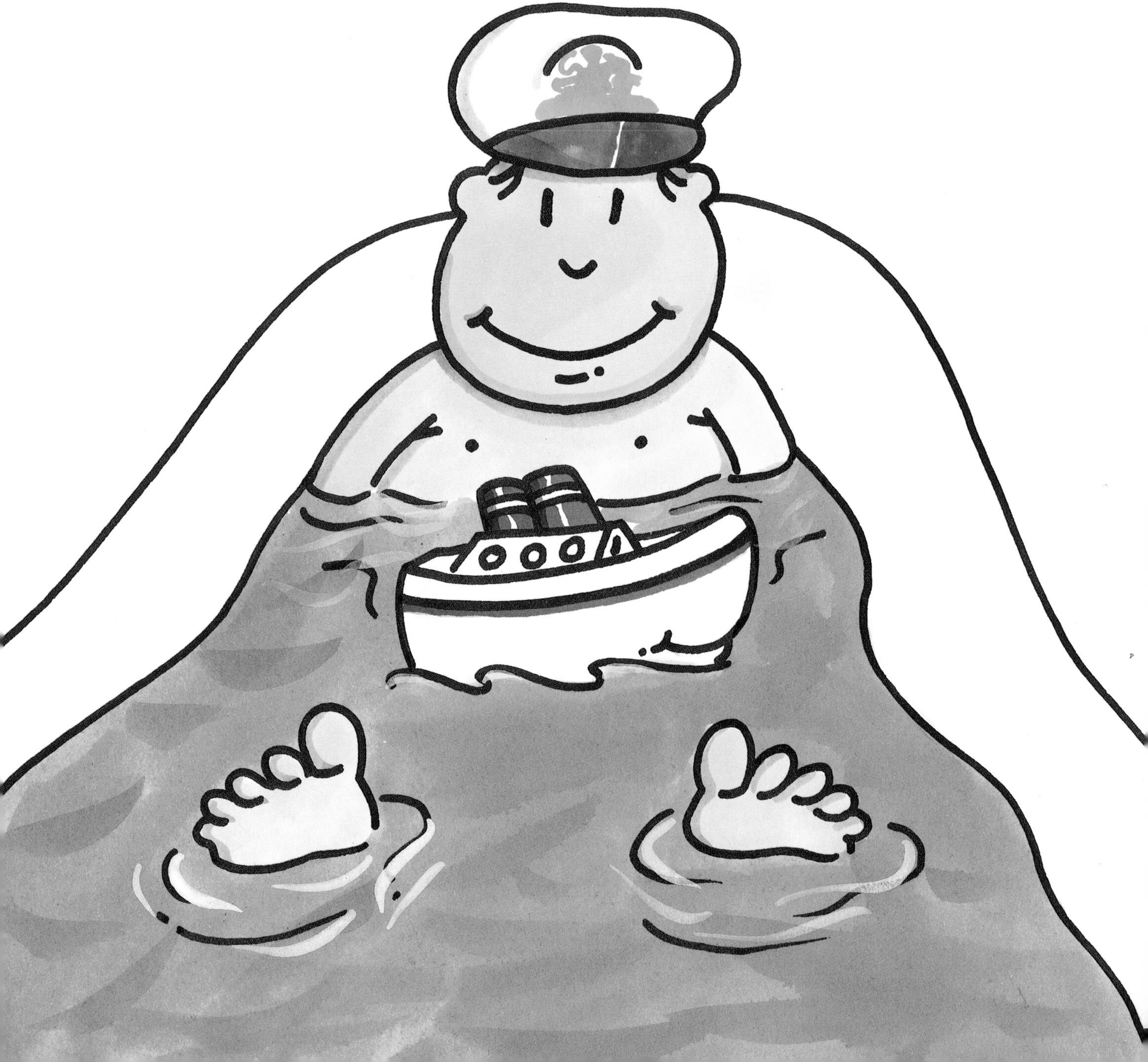

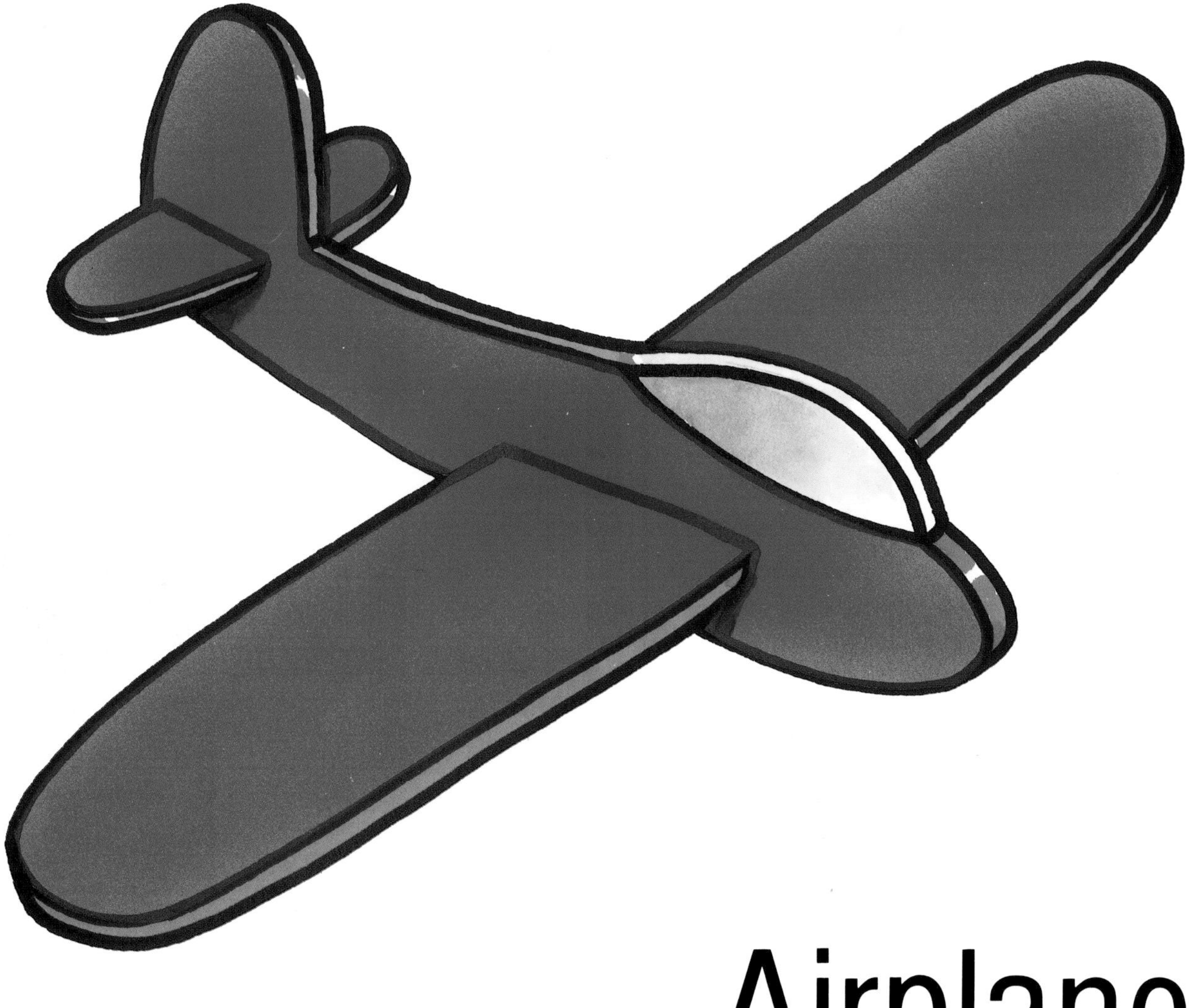

Airplane

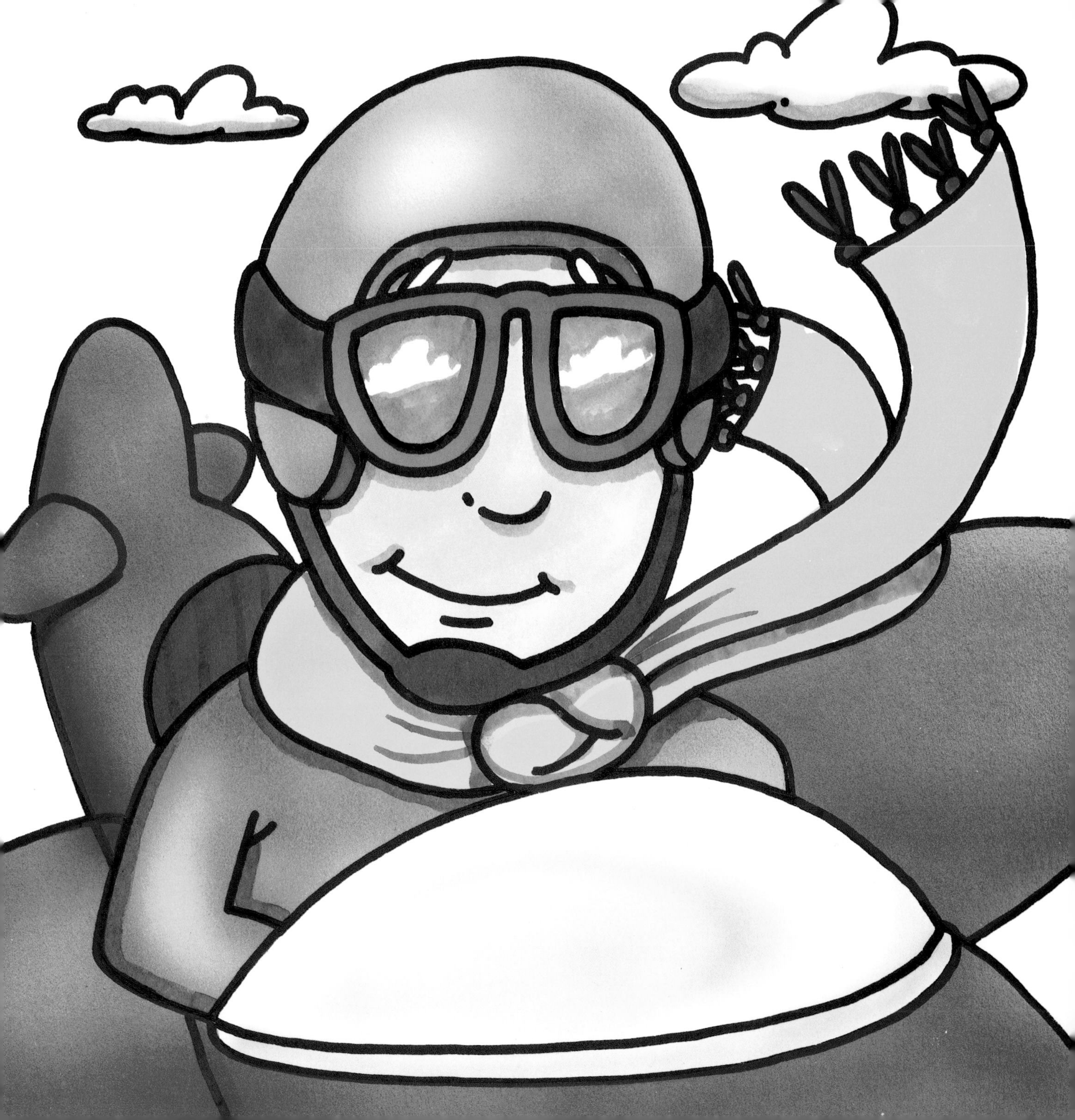

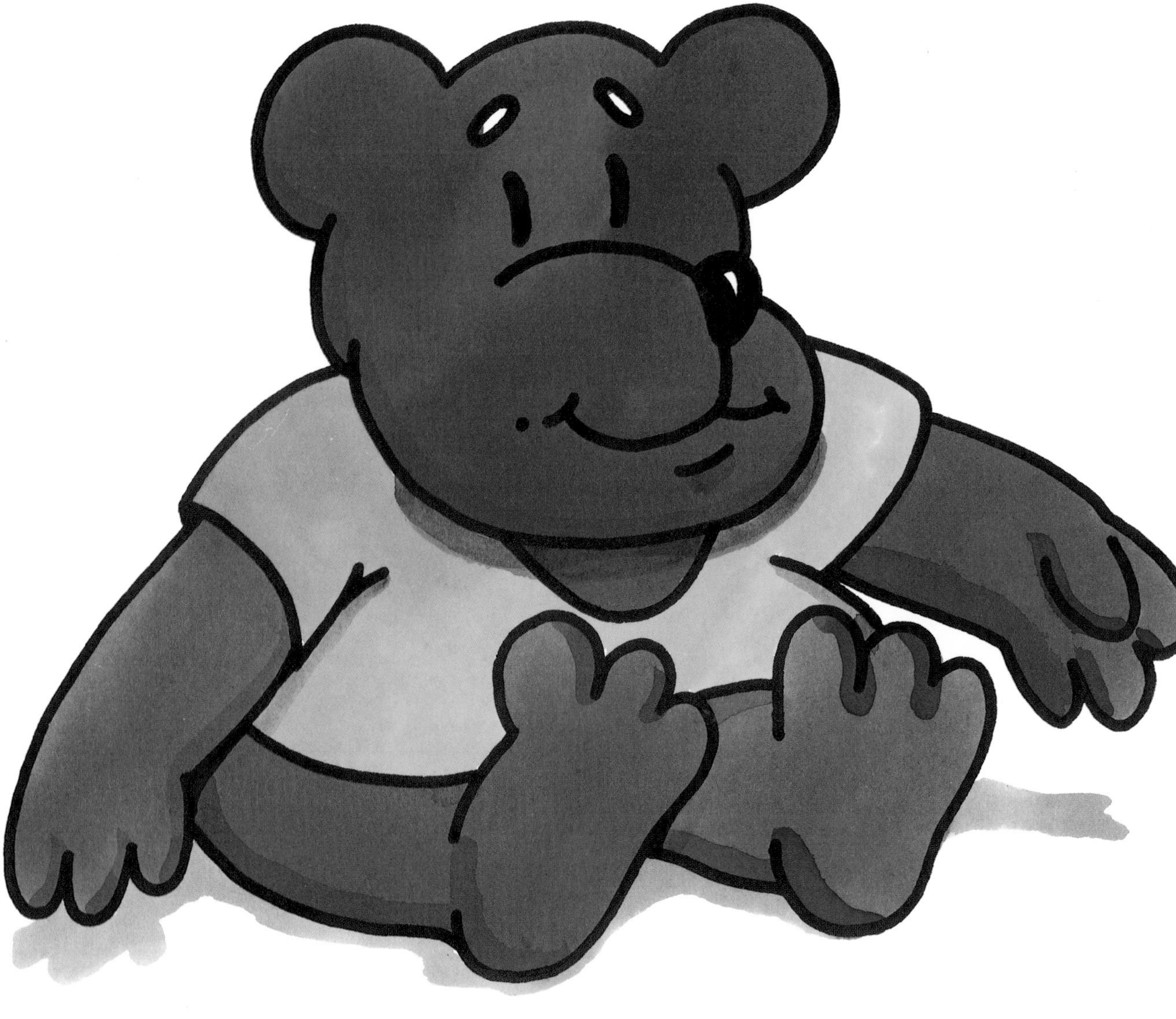

Teddy Bear

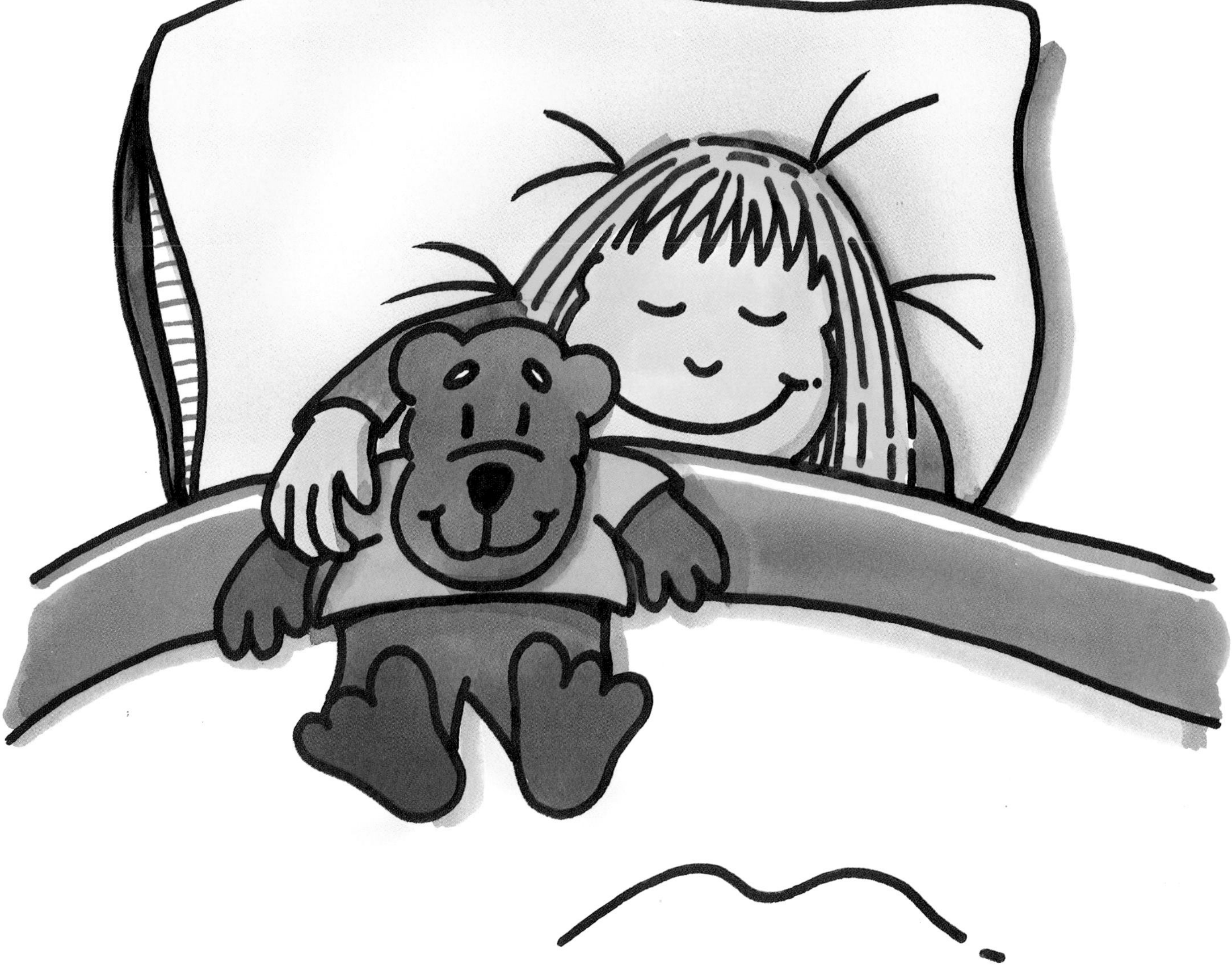

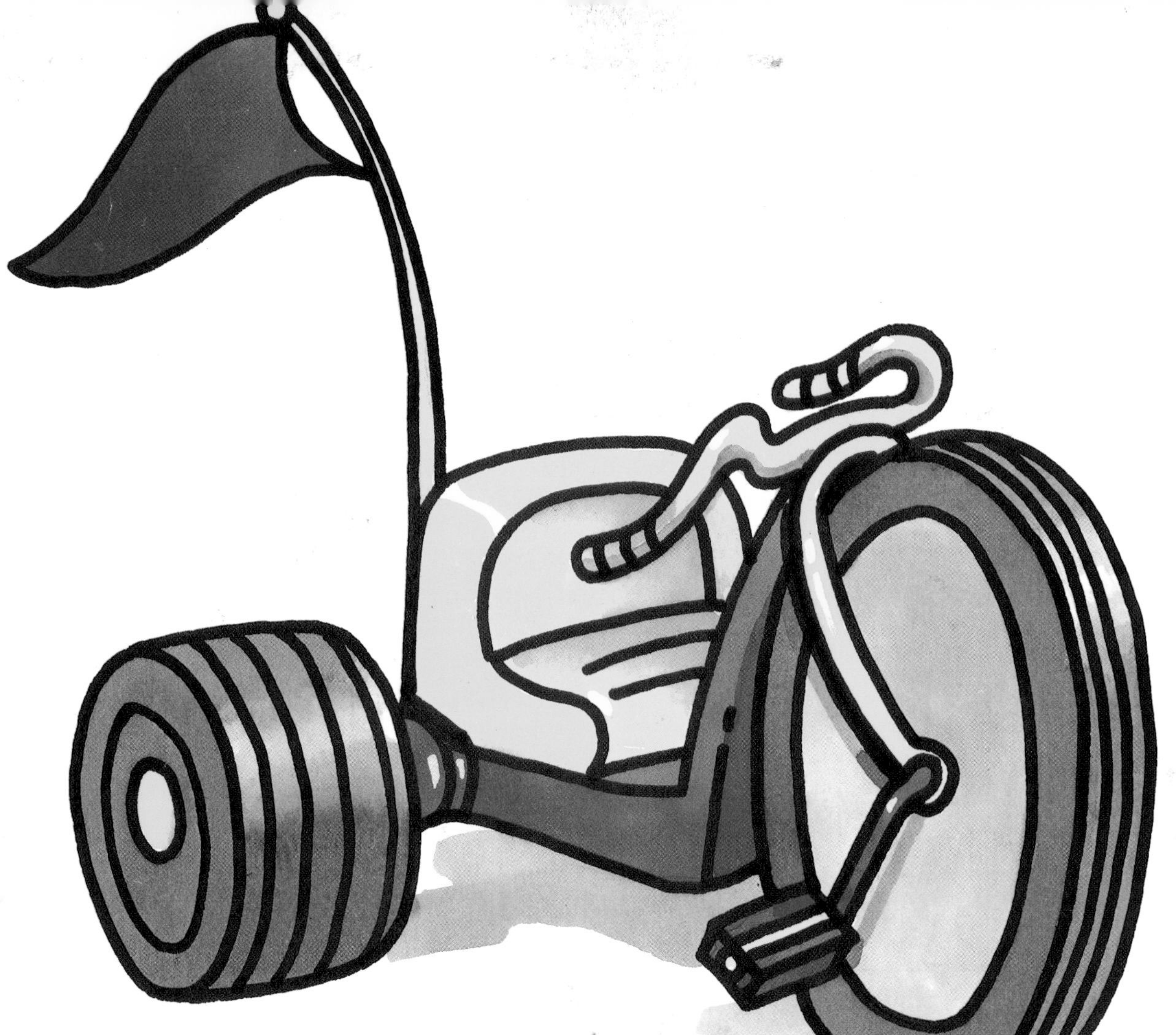

Tricycle